Wharton Executive
EDUCATION ESSENTIALS

Customer
Centricity

Also Available

Wharton Executive Education Finance &
Accounting Essentials,
by Richard A. Lambert

For more information,
visit wdp.wharton.upenn.edu

Wharton Executive
EDUCATION ESSENTIALS

Customer Centricity

What It Is, What It Isn't, and Why It Matters

Peter Fader

Wharton
DIGITAL PRESS
Philadelphia

Published by Wharton Digital Press
The Wharton School
University of Pennsylvania
3620 Locust Walk
2000 Steinberg Hall-Dietrich Hall
Philadelphia, PA 19104

Ebook ISBN: 978-1-61363-008-2
Paperback ISBN: 978-1-61363-007-5

Design by Charles Kreloff Design, Inc.

Contents

Introduction

L et's start in Fairbanks, Alaska. Specifically, at the Fairbanks location of one of the most successful brands in retail: Nordstrom.

Nordstrom is a high-end retailer that, of course, sells many wonderful products. But as we all know, Nordstrom is not really famous for *what* it sells; it is famous for *how* it sells—with truly outstanding customer service. Nordstrom is known far and wide as the most customer-friendly retailer in the business, and that reputation is richly deserved. It's also no fluke. Indeed, the company to this very day gives all new employees a one-page company handbook that very simply states, "Our number one goal is to provide outstanding customer service."

Nordstrom executives *demand* outstanding customer service. And their employees deliver it. That's why Nordstrom sends thank-you cards to its customers. That's why Nordstrom clerks walk all the way around their counters to hand shoppers their bags. And that's also why, more often than not, if you ask to return an item to Nordstrom, your request will be granted.

Which brings us back to Fairbanks and one of the most well-worn tales in all of business history—the Nordstrom tire story.

According to legend, the year was 1975, and an unhappy owner of a set of worn-down tires walked into the new Alaskan Nordstrom outpost and asked to return them. The request was an odd one for several reasons, the most notable being this: Nordstrom not only did not sell the man the tires in question, but also *did not sell tires at all.*

No matter, the story goes; the store granted the request anyway. And all at once, Nordstrom had a handy little story on which to hang its customer-service hat. Indeed, in the years since this story originated, company spokespeople have on several different occasions backed its authenticity.

Of course, why wouldn't they? Every retailer wants to be known as customer friendly. Every retailer wants to be trusted. Every retailer wants to be known as the store that not only *says* the customer is always right, but actually *believes* the customer is always right. Nordstrom, apparently, is precisely that company.

But here's what you need to understand: Nordstrom was probably wrong to do this.

Despite everything you may have ever learned about business; despite all that you've been told about customer relations by your bosses, peers, and mentors; and despite even your gut instinct, I am here to let you in on this little secret: *the customer is not always right.*

Rather, the *right* customers are always right. And yes, there is a difference.

Not All Customers Are Created Equal

This is not a book about customer service. This is not a book about being customer friendly, either. This is a book about customer centricity. And although you may be surprised to hear it, there is nothing inherently customer centric about Nordstrom taking back a set of tires that they didn't sell in the first place.

As you'll learn in *Wharton Executive Education Customer Centricity Essentials*, customer centricity is not really about being nice to your customers. It is not a philosophy. It is not something that can be fostered through a company handbook or mission statement.

Customer centricity is a *strategy* to fundamentally align a company's products and services with the wants and needs of its most valuable customers. That strategy has a specific aim: more profits for the long term.

This is a goal that every business would like to achieve, of course. And it's a goal that your company can achieve as well. But you'll only be able to get there and put customer centricity to use if you are willing to start thinking in new—and in some cases, truly radical—ways. That starts with scrapping some old ideas about company-customer relations, and it continues with a willingness to radically rethink organizational design, performance metrics, product development, and more—all in the name of finding new and unique ways of serving the customers who matter most.

The way I see things—and the way I want you to start seeing things—is that not all customers are created equal. Not all customers deserve your company's best efforts. And despite what that the tired old adage says, the customer is most definitely not always right. Because in the world of customer centricity, there are good customers . . . and then there is everybody else.

That latter group shouldn't be ignored, of course. I'm not suggesting that you ditch them, treat them shabbily, or ignore their wants and needs. I am suggesting, however, that you would be well served—and so would your stockholders—if you started spending more of your time working with the former group. Those are the customers who hold the key to your company's long-term profitability.

Customer centricity is about identifying your most valuable customers—and then doing everything in your power to make as much money from them as possible and to find more customers like them. These customers give you a strategic advantage over your competitors; it's a strategic advantage that could be the best path forward for many companies.

This is something that airlines and hotels have long understood. It's something Amazon, the massive (and creative) online retailer, has understood almost from the very start, way back in 1994. Wells Fargo understands the importance of customer centricity. So, too, do the executives who run Harrah's casinos; the powers-that-be at IBM; and maybe most especially, the leaders of British retailer Tesco, who state very openly that the data they gather from their customer-centric initiatives drive every major strategic decision they make. As this list suggests, there is great variety in the types of companies (and industries) that have put customer-centric practices into use, but these customer-centric savvy companies are hardly in the majority; they are the exception, not the rule.

Although the idea of customer centricity has been around for years (decades, really, as you'll learn later in this chapter) and although customer centricity has been proven in practice to be an incredibly effective means of maximizing customer lifetime value (you'll learn more about this later also), a shocking number of really well-run companies still don't seem the least bit interested in building a customer-centric culture, even though doing so would very clearly be to their benefit.

Costco, which has been helping its customers save pennies for years, isn't truly customer centric. Apple, which was recently named as the most valuable brand in the world, isn't customer centric—at least not yet. Walmart isn't customer centric. Starbucks isn't customer centric. And no matter what your gut may tell you, Nordstrom—sainted, famously customer-friendly Nordstrom—isn't truly customer centric, either.

A Path to Customer Centricity

The aim of *Wharton Executive Education Customer Centricity Essentials* is simple: to give you a clear and concise understanding of what customer centricity is and isn't; to help you understand why a customer-centric outlook might prove crucial to your bottom-line success in today's superfast, supercompetitive environment; and to guide you around the pitfalls that other companies have faced when attempting to implement customer-centric initiatives.

The topics I'll cover include the following:

- Why the traditional means of doing business— the product-centric approach—is more vulnerable than ever before.

- How the strategies underlying customer centricity can help companies gain a competitive advantage in today's challenging business environment.

- How some cutting-edge companies and leading business minds are rethinking the idea of equity— and how the ideas of brand equity and customer equity help us understand what kinds of companies naturally lend themselves to the customer-centric model and which ones don't.

- Why the traditional models for determining the value of individual customers (something we call customer lifetime value, or CLV) are flawed—and how a rather simple tweak to that model can deliver a much more accurate picture of what individual customers and entire customer bases are really worth.

- How executives can use CLV and other customer-centric data to make smarter decisions about their companies.

- How the well-intended idea of customer relationship management (CRM) lost its way—and how your company can properly put CRM to use.

This book will give you the knowledge and tools you need to succeed in a world that, in the years to come, may well *demand* a customer-centric approach. In other words, by the time you're done reading this book, you'll be ahead of the game. It's a game that has been in the works for decades now. In fact, I should point out that there is nothing necessarily new about customer centricity—or at the very least, nothing new about the ideas on which it is built. The roots of customer centricity can be traced all the way back to the late 1960s, when a relatively obscure ad agency executive by the name of Lester Wunderman gave birth to the idea that we know today as direct marketing. Many of the concepts you'll read about in this book, including the basic overarching notion that businesses would be well served to know absolutely everything about their best customers, are derived in some way from the ideas of Wunderman, who understood long before anyone else the value of keeping records (frighteningly detailed records, actually) about customer buying habits.

What is new, however, is the competitive landscape and the incredibly demanding world in which you and your company are doing business. Today, more than ever before, many companies *need* customer centricity. They need it to compete in the short term and thrive in the long term.

The world has changed dramatically in the decades since Henry Ford first proved the viability of the tried-and-true product-centric business model—the model we'll explore in detail in chapter 1. That model worked wonderfully in the 1920s, and indeed, it still works pretty well today. It is not my contention that the product-centric model is broken; rather, I simply believe the product-centric model is no longer *enough* in many situations.

Technology, deregulation, globalization, and other factors have conspired to rob even the most wildly successful product-centric companies of the full set of inherent advantages that used to arise automatically from a well-executed product-centric strategy. Technological barriers have been broken down. Geographic barriers are all but nonexistent. But what remains are the relationships that companies have—or don't have—with their customers.

Most companies have been able to get by without customer centricity in the past. Many may be able to get by without customer centricity today. And some will be able to get by without customer centricity for years to come. But *most* companies in *most* sectors probably won't be able to get by without customer centricity forever, so they might as well start moving in this direction sooner rather than later.

I believe the companies that will enjoy the most success in the years and decades to come will be the companies that dedicate the resources necessary to not only understand their most loyal and committed customers, but also make the effort to then serve these valuable customers—and serve them in a way that will not only make them feel special but also maximize their value to the company. Make no mistake: your competitors want to steal your customers, and some of those competitors may be plotting at this very moment to do precisely that. Maybe, like National Car

Rental, they are creating a unique customer loyalty program that will allow them to serve their customers more efficiently than anyone else in the marketplace. Maybe, like Harrah's casinos, they have come to the understanding that although they might not be able to compete on sheer size, they can compete with kindness—that is, "kindness" delivered via a sophisticated patron-tracking program that ensures each customer visit to a Harrah's floor is a *profitable* visit.

Or maybe, having just heard the famous Nordstrom tire story for the umpteenth time, your competitor's top executive is starting to reconsider her strategy by asking whether that Nordstrom clerk's kindly action— the decision to take those tires back even though Nordstrom didn't sell the tires in the first place— actually made any sense. In the realm of customer centricity, at least, it's a question that can only be answered if one is given the right information—the kind of information that customer-centric companies use every single day to identify, serve, and leverage their best customers and maximize profits. Was the tire guy a regular Nordstrom shopper? If so, how often did he stop by—and how much did he spend? Was he really committed to Nordstrom? What was his business really worth? And if it turned out that business was worth a lot (or not much at all), well, what then? Accepting that bizarre return request may have been a good public relations decision, judged by the wisdom of hindsight. But it probably wasn't a good business decision.

In this book, you'll learn how and why those questions should be asked and answered. I'll explain where customer centricity came from, how it evolved into its current form, and the advantages it holds in a changing marketplace—a marketplace still dominated, at least for now, by companies holding fast to the product-centric model. I'll take a look at successful customer-centric companies, explore the "paradox" of customer centricity, and guide you around some potential challenges en route to customer-centric success.

By the time you are finished with *Wharton Executive Education Customer Centricity Essentials*, you'll understand all of the basics of the customer-centric model— what it is, how it works, and how you can use it to maximize your profits. You'll also understand, as I do, that Nordstrom was probably wrong to take back those tires in 1975.

Chapter 1

Product Centricity: Cracks in the Foundation

In this chapter:

- What is product centricity?
- Why are there cracks in the foundation of product centricity?
- Why does being customer friendly fall short of being truly customer centric?

What Is Product Centricity?

What is the primary objective of *every* company in *every* sector and *every* marketplace in the world?

Well, the answer is obvious, isn't it? The only reason anyone goes into business—the only reason any commercial enterprise exists—is to make a profit and to maximize those profits over as long a time period as possible. We are in business to make money. Preferably, a lot of it. And broadly speaking, for the better part of the past century, all companies have used the same general strategy to achieve that goal. That strategy can be termed "product centricity."

Ever since Henry Ford introduced the world to the

wonders of the assembly line, companies of all kinds, even service firms, have followed that same path to growth and profitability. Ford's model—the product-centric model—worked. And it worked because of the virtuous cycle that underpinned the entire thing. As Ford understood when he unveiled the Model-T back in 1908, and as companies today still understand, the more products you sell, the cheaper it becomes to manufacture those products, which means you can make more products, sell more of them, and make even more money.

The product-centric model is precisely what the name suggests. Organizations that follow this model are literally built, from top to bottom, around the demands of the product:

- All strategic advantage is based on the product and the product expertise behind those products.

- Divisions and teams are set up around products.

- Employees are rewarded based on their ability to create new products or sell existing products.

- The long-term focus is about strengthening the product portfolio and constantly finding new ways to expand it.

- The brand is perceived to have greater value than the customer.

Create a product, market a product, sell a product. Repeat.

It's a time-tested and well-proven approach to business, so it's no surprise that 99% of companies on the planet still operate this way today. It doesn't matter if they are selling widgets or consulting services or plastic surgery or education; most business executives view the world through the lens of product centricity. It's hard to blame them. Indeed, as Apple, Walmart, and Coca-Cola prove, the product-centric ways of Henry Ford can still deliver the profits. Product centricity can still win your company massive market share. Product centricity can still make your company a global powerhouse.

And here's the thing: Product centricity is pretty simple.

Profits are maximized through volume and market share, and volume and market share are driven by growth—growth derived, generally speaking, in one of two ways. Companies can either expand their reach into new markets—demographic, geographic, or otherwise—or they can tweak an existing product just enough to convince their customers that version 2.0 really is that much better than version 1.0. The viability of the former method is self-explanatory. And although the latter is a bit more complicated, it continues to be a proven winner as well. Consumers like the new and improved. They like the latest. And companies are happy to deliver precisely that, especially when it is highly cost effective to do so.

So yes, market expansion works. New product development and line extensions work too. And as a result, product centricity works. Through the proven, reliable, and very much alive-and-kicking product-centric approach, companies are achieving exactly what they want to achieve: profits. In some cases, they are achieving enormous profits.

Take a look at Apple—possibly the most successful product company in existence today. Despite the continued health issues faced by Steve Jobs, the company's founder and creative force, Apple kicked off fiscal year 2011 with the single-best quarterly performance in company history. Apple sold 4.1 million Macs that quarter (nearly 25% more than they had in the previous year) along with 16.3 million iPhones, 19.45 million iPods, and 7.33 million iPads. Revenues reached $26.74 billion. Profits topped $6 billion. Revenues were up 71% and earnings were up 78% from the previous year. Right now, Apple is dominating its marketplace. A recent study by the marketing research firm Millward Brown estimated that the Apple brand is worth over $150 billion. Who can argue with that kind of success?

In that sense, Jobs and the powers-that-be in Cupertino, California, have no reason to change. No reason at all.

At least not yet.

Why Are There Cracks in the Foundation of Product Centricity?

I have two teenage children, so I can speak with authority when I say today's kids are spoiled. They are the most demanding generation the world has ever seen. They know exactly what they want, and because they have no patience whatsoever, they want what they want immediately. And they don't care how they get what they want, as long as they get it when they want it and in the format they want it.

The lesson for your company is obvious. Maybe you've got these kids as customers today. But unless you are prepared to meet their every demand *tomorrow*, they may not be your customers for long. In the parlance of sports, these kids are "free agents." Their loyalty extends as far as their next passing whim.

In this regard, the modern teenager is quite emblematic of the changing face of the business world. It is a business world that, in my view, is becoming less forgiving of the product-centric model and more demanding of a customer-centric model—a model based not on expertise in the realm of product development, but rather on a deep understanding of what customers actually want, when and how they want it, and what they're willing to give you in exchange.

The rules of the game have changed, and consumers hold far more power than ever before in today's ultracompetitive business environment. Make no mistake: although the product-centric model is not quite broken, there are certainly some cracks in the foundation. Those cracks can be traced to four key factors:

1. Technological advances and the speed with which new technologies are created and copied.

2. Globalization and the geographic advantages that have been lost as a result.

3. Deregulation and the way it has shaken up traditionally stable industries.

4. The rising power of the consumer and their newfound ability to get what they want, whenever they want, from whomever they want.

These trends have reshaped the world of business—and they should not be ignored.

For the better part of the past century, a well-run product-centric company essentially operated with a stacked deck; they enjoyed an inherent strategic advantage specifically because of their product expertise. If that company had superior technology, their market share was fairly secure. And if that company had locked down their geographic marketplace—or at the very least was located far enough from would-be competitors to make their competition irrelevant—their position was even more secure. These days, neither advantage truly exists. At least not in the way they used to exist.

Because of the near incomprehensible pace of technological advance these days, and because of the spread of technological knowledge to all corners of the globe, there is a much smaller technological advantage in business than ever before. Whatever you invent today can be knocked off tomorrow. So whereas it used to be true that a top-performing product or a truly cutting-edge technology could reign supreme, without competition, for years and years, that window of dominance has been shaved to months, weeks, and even days. This trend is probably most prominent in the computing space, where it is both clichéd and undeniably true that a computer is obsolete almost from the moment it is purchased.

Meanwhile, globalization—the borderless reality in which business operates today—has wiped away almost every company's geographic advantage as well. Those ever-more demanding consumers of today have good reason to be demanding; the entire world, and all of its goods and services, is now at their fingertips— and where a product is manufactured is essentially irrelevant. The product from China is as available to them as the product from their hometown, and in this sense, every company, no matter where it's located and no matter what its business, is competing in a truly global marketplace.

Everything is now everywhere, all at once. Consumers are smarter than ever before. The market is more saturated than ever before, more competitive than ever before, and changing more quickly than ever before. It is the perfect storm, and it explains why today's teens—and many adults—are so demanding: they can be. Because of technology and globalization and deregulation and the sheer speed at which business can and does get done, we have gotten to the point where consumers have all of the choices— and by extension, all of the power. So although I can justifiably be frustrated by just how easy my kids have it these days, the reality is that they have every right to be demanding. The market has declared it so.

So where does this leave product-centric companies? Well, in my view, it leaves them vulnerable. Or at the very least, more vulnerable than ever before to their competition—competition that is coming at them from all angles, on all fronts, and from every corner of the globe.

Which brings me to one last important change in the world of business. Just as technology has made life more difficult for businesses, so too has it created wonderful new opportunities. When Lester Wunderman, that underappreciated genius, literally coined the phrase "direct marketing" back in November of 1967, he had little to work with. He had his ideas. He had customers. And he had a bunch of pens and a few

stacks of index cards. That's about it. Any information that Wunderman or his clients collected about
their customers had to be gathered the old-fashioned
way—by putting pen to paper. Wunderman taught
client firms how (and why) to document every point of
contact between the direct marketer and its customers,
and he slowly but surely built what must have seemed
at the time to be a fairly enormous database.

Today, that same database can be built in a few key-
strokes. Today, for the first time in history, companies
can collect massive amounts of data—once unthink-
able amounts of data, really—about their customers.
Important data. Actionable data. They can know what
their customers buy and when they buy it and where
they buy it and more. The data are there. And you
know what? Some really smart companies—Amazon
being possibly the most notable example—are leveraging that data, often with enormous success.

This data explosion is the last crack in the foundation and possibly the most important reason why the
product-centric model is imperiled. Customer-level
data are more available to you today than ever been
before. And if you don't use it, your competitors will.

Why Does Being Customer Friendly Fall Short of Being Truly Customer Centric?

Starting in the next chapter, we will begin to explore exactly what customer centricity *is*—its definition, the organizational and cultural changes that it demands, and why I believe this new model really is the future of business. But first I should draw a line in the sand and explain, once and for all, what customer centricity *isn't*. This is an important distinction to make.

I now teach a regular course on customer centricity at the Wharton School, and in the first lecture of each semester, I put my students through a little exercise. Right after I explain what product centricity is, and right after I explain why I think product centricity is more vulnerable than ever before, I play a little trick on them. I put up a slide that lists five companies known far and wide for their customer orientation: Nordstrom, Walmart, Apple, Costco, and Starbucks. Then I run down the list, one by one, and poll students on whether they believe each company is customer centric. The responses always amuse me because each and every semester it becomes readily apparent that even the brightest students all too easily confuse customer service with customer centricity.

When that slide goes up, my students extol the customer-friendly virtues of Starbucks. They rave about how Walmart and Costco can deliver just about any product on Earth at precisely the right price to their customers. They speak in mild awe about storied old Nordstrom. And of course, they agree pretty much across the board that Apple—beloved, trendy Apple— loves its customers almost as much as its customers love Apple. And then they look at me in great bewilderment as I inform them that *none* of those companies is actually customer centric. Not customer centric enough, at least.

Let me explain why.

Let's start with Walmart and Costco. Walmart now has nearly 9,000 stores in 15 countries around the world, and Costco reported revenues of nearly $9 billion in 2011. Although Walmart and Costco are undoubtedly successful, they aren't customer centric; the reality is that despite their massive sales numbers and retail sector dominance, both companies are flying blind when it comes to their individual customers. Their model is utterly and completely product centric, even though they don't make their own products. Both retailers stock their shelves full of products—an unmatched variety of products—and then sell them cheaper than almost anyone else can. That's about the extent of it. And yes, it has worked out fairly well.

But how do these firms collect and leverage customer-level data? How well do they sort out their best customers from the rest of the pack? Not particularly well at all. In fact, they don't even try to do so. Are you a member of the Walmart loyalty program? Of course not; they don't have one. Why? Because it wouldn't be cost effective for them to take on all that overhead. (This is also true for many other retailers who *do* have loyalty programs, but that's another matter.) Walmart is very good at knowing which kinds of products should be sold in which geographic areas at which times, but they have no idea about the wants and needs—and lifetime value—of any individual customer. One notable exception is their Walmart.com subsidiary, but this division is a small part of the overall company, and they are generally unable to match online purchases with offline purchases made by the same household.

Costco, in contrast, collects that data as part of their regular operations because all customers must use their membership cards at checkout. But it's not clear what they do with all this rich data. Like Walmart, they are superb at making aggregate decisions about which products to sell where and when, but they make little or no effort to target individuals with customized offers. Why?

Both firms are paragons of product centricity. They sell in huge volumes and keep their costs wonderfully low. It's just not worth their while to start sorting out one customer from another—at least not yet, anyway.

Similar questions can be raised about Nordstrom, albeit to a lesser extent. On one level, Nordstrom seems to very deeply understand the value of its customers—yet on another level, they still fall short of customer-centric success. Yes, it is true that Nordstrom will take back used tires that it didn't even sell in the first place. Yes, it is true that Nordstrom clerks will walk around the counter to hand you your bag to save you the effort of lifting your arms. And yes, it is true that Nordstrom executives stress the importance of customer service possibly more than any other executives at any other retailer on the planet. Which is all fine and good.

But as a regular Nordstrom shopper, I wonder how much they know about me—and why they don't try to have a conversation that reflects my long and deep history of transactions with them. Individual sales people remember me and my previous purchases in their department, but this information doesn't seem to be tied together into a single comprehensive profile of me. In other words, they don't know what I am worth. I am nameless. Faceless. I am "the customer"—one of millions, whom they treat well in the store, just like all the rest. I wonder if Nordstrom as a company has any idea how often I shop there or what I buy when I do. Would they know enough about me to decide how much my lifetime value would be impacted if they did (or didn't) take back a set of tires that I wished to return there? I doubt it.

Starbucks is another example of a customer-friendly operation that falls short of customer centricity. Millions of people around the world start their day with a trip to their neighborhood Starbucks. Many of them order the same drink every day, without fail. And certainly, it can be assumed that, at their local Starbucks at least, the baristas know exactly what these customers want. But what happens when those extremely loyal Starbucks customers hit the road? What are the chances that the baristas in Kansas City will know as much about that customer as the staffers back home in Philadelphia? Can you walk into any random Starbucks and say, "I'll have the usual, please"? I don't think so. Starbucks makes almost no effort to learn anything about its customers. It offers no consistent customer loyalty program (despite many failed efforts to start one). It gathers virtually zero data at the customer level. It simply delivers its product—and hopes that's enough. Starbucks, it seems to me, is leaving huge amounts of money on the table by failing to take advantage of the deeply ingrained buying habits that many of its customers have established over the years.

And finally, let's discuss much-loved Apple. When I poll my students more hands go up as affirmation of Apple's presumed customer centricity than for any of the other firms. The company is a marvel at anticipating and shaping customer preferences, then profiting from these insights thanks to its unique abilities to design, manufacture, distribute, and promote its products. Apple has deservedly leapt to the forefront of the computing world. The company has evolved into a powerhouse. More than that, the company is a marketer's dream. Apple is trendy, hip, and enormously popular among young people, and it is supported by a legion of fans who are loyal beyond all measure of loyalty. Apple people are truly *all in* for Apple. And it is certainly true that the company goes out of its way to treat its fans pretty well; as my son can attest, if your iPod breaks, the good folks at the Apple Store will treat you wonderfully while you await your repairs.

But again—and I cannot emphasize this enough—*that's not really the point of customer centricity.*

For as much as Apple appears to care about its customers, the company has thus far taken only modest steps—surprisingly modest steps, actually—to really *understand* those customers. And the reason is simple: for all of its hipness, and for all of its cutting-edge credibility, the truth is that Apple is a pretty old-school operation. In fact, it's one of the most product-centric operations on the scene today. And I say that with enormous respect for how they do it.

Product centricity is how Steve Jobs built the company in the first place, and product centricity is the way the company continues to operate to this very day. The folks at Apple are geniuses when it comes to design and new product development. They are remarkably adept at coming up with new things, endlessly versioning those new things, and of course, convincing their customers to buy those new things. In that respect, Steve Jobs has utterly perfected Henry Ford's old model: develop a product, market a product, sell a product, *repeat.*

Millions upon millions of people buy Apple's products every single month. The company has countless opportunities to engage with those customers, learn from them, understand them. But what does Apple do to actually achieve this? What does the company *really* know about each of those millions of people who so anxiously await each and every new product offering? Surprisingly, it knows very little.

For proof, look no further than iTunes, which despite its massive popularity and industry-shaping influence was actually quite late to the party for something as basic as a recommendation engine. The Genius engine, which uses past purchase history to tell customers what other songs they may like, didn't arrive until 2008. That's a stunningly delayed response, especially considering the fact that Amazon had been doing basically the same thing for more than 10 years.

Again, I am not here to tell you that the folks at Apple don't know what they're doing. I'm not here to say their model doesn't work, because it quite clearly works just fine. But I am here to say that even enormously successful companies like Apple will eventually need to start thinking in new ways, questioning the status quo, and wondering what comes next. They need to ask themselves, in other words, whether that old model—the product-centric model that has so dominated business for so very long—will be as viable and as profitable in 5 or 10 years as it is today. Because I'll be honest: I have my doubts. Product centricity has worked for Apple and many other companies for a long time, and product centricity is still working for them now. But it won't work forever—because *just* having the best product, the best service, or the best technology won't always be enough.

The world has changed, and companies must change with it.

Chapter 2

Customer Centricity: The New Model for Success

In this chapter:

- What is customer centricity?
- What are the challenges associated with customer centricity?
- The paradox of customer centricity: what about your other customers?

What Is Customer Centricity?

Before answering this question, I must emphasize a particular point because it's an important one. The ultimate aim of the customer-centric model is the same as the ultimate aim of the product-centric model: to make the company as profitable as possible in the long run. All of the ideas that you'll read about in this book—all of the terminologies and methodologies and theories of customer centricity—are simply a means to an end. That end is profitability—long-term profitability, that is. In that way, a customer-centric approach to business is no different than a product-centric approach to business.

This raises an obvious question. If the end goal is the same, and if the end goal is to make money, then why are so many companies—and so many executives and managers—so skeptical of customer centricity? Why do they cling to the product-centric past? Well, the answer is simple. They are skeptical of customer centricity because so much of what the model calls for is so unconventional—and because a great deal of what customer centricity entails flies right in the face of some long-held business beliefs.

Yes, the *ends* of customer centricity may be conventional; the *means* of customer centricity, however, are radical. And in the end, putting customer centricity into practice demands a good bit of work—and a willingness to suffer a short-term hit in the pursuit of long-term gain.

In this chapter, we are going to begin exploring exactly what customer centricity is, how it works, and how many companies can implement customer-centric strategies to bolster profits and long-term viability. We'll also take a look at the "paradox" of customer centricity and figure out what we do with all of those customers who don't fit the profile of the all-important right customers.

For now, let's start with the basics—a definition of customer centricity:

Customer centricity is a strategy that aligns a company's development and delivery of its products and services with the current and future needs of a select set of customers in order to maximize their long-term financial value to the firm.

We will be discussing the many nuances of this definition throughout the book, but that one sentence is basically customer centricity in a nutshell: a fundamental acknowledgment that not all customers are created equal; a commitment to identify those customers who matter most; and a willingness to dedicate disproportionate amounts of resources not only to understand what those customers want but to deliver what they want—and by extension, create a stable, lucrative, and ever-more profitable future.

Only a few smart companies—Amazon, IBM, Harrah's, Tesco, and Netflix, to name a few—are practicing customer centricity. Why is this? Why do so many companies seem so reluctant to make this strategic leap forward? I think the issue is quite simple. Customer centricity requires that a company be willing and able to change its organizational design, performance metrics, and employee and distributor structures to focus on this long-term creation and delivery process.

This may not seem all that revolutionary at first, but this definition and its requirements are really quite radical—specifically, because it spells out just how drmatically customer centricity differs from (and clashes with) the old tried-and-true product-centric model. The challenges that come along with the adoption of a truly customer-centric approach are not insignificant. Customer centricity requires major organizational, structural, strategic, and cultural changes.

What Are the Challenges Associated with Customer Centricity?

There is one overarching reason why customer centricity demands such sweeping organizational change, and that reason goes right back to the daring, radical idea that not all customers are created equal and therefore should not and cannot be *treated* as equals. It's an idea we will come back to again and again.

In my definition of customer centricity, the customer-centric way of doing business specifically calls on organizations to identify a select set of customers. These are the important ones, the lucrative ones, the ones you should be spending your time thinking about, planning around, producing and working for—the right customers. These are the customers who matter.

Of course, in the product-centric world, there are no right customers. There is no dividing line between the important ones and the rest. They are all just customers—the nameless, faceless hordes who gobble up (or ignore) whatever it is Company X is attempting to sell.

One of my favorite anecdotes about this point dates back to the early 2000s, when the energy sector was just beginning the deregulation process. Around that time, I had the opportunity to work with some energy firms, and I remember being struck by the unique language they used to describe their customers. Energy firms didn't call them "customers" at all. They called them "rate-payers." Now, if that doesn't speak volumes about how old-school energy firms viewed their customers—as homogenous, slavish, unthinking sources of revenue—I don't know what does.

The scary thing is, those power companies were (and are) hardly alone. Just think for moment about how many times you've heard companies or executives talk about "the customer" in business plans, in shareholder presentations, in the business press. That dreaded phrase is utterly ubiquitous, but I've got some news for you. *"The customer" does not exist because every customer is different.*

Customer-centric firms acknowledge the heterogeneity among our customers. More than that, we *celebrate* it—because we understand that heterogeneity offers us opportunity. In a customer-centric company, we understand that some customers do matter more. We understand that some customers do deserve more—and by extension, some customers deserve *less*. We understand that it's okay to give them less. I really believe that. I believe it very deeply, in fact. But I also understand this idea is pretty far out there—and I understand the enormous challenge associated with its real-world implementation.

It's a challenge that organizations must tackle on both the organizational and financial fronts.

The Organizational Challenge

The idea that some customers matter more than others is a radical one. But so is the idea that your company should completely retool its research and development functions, rework its metrics, and generally rethink every aspect of its daily operations specifically to meet the demands of those right customers—and in the process acknowledge that your old way of doing things was, for lack of a better term, misguided.

So many companies are so good at the product-centric basics—inventing a thing, producing a thing, delivering a thing, inventing a new thing, and so on—that they don't stop to ask themselves, even for a moment, whether the customers they are selling to are the right ones. In a customer-centric firm, however, that question gets asked repeatedly because customer centricity flips the model. Companies don't make and sell the products they *think* their customers will want; they make and sell products they *know* their customers will want. It's a fundamentally different way of doing business, and one that requires quite a bit of effort up front to separate the right customers from the wrong ones.

Once you have identified your right customers the next steps are obvious. You mine those customers for information. You find out what they want, what they need, and what they will demand going forward. You find out how to acquire new customers who share some of the key characteristics that distinguish your best customers. And then you position your company, from the very top of the corporate structure right down to the on-the-ground sales force, to deliver on these ideas—because by identifying and serving those customers (and in some sense ignoring the rest), you will be doing precisely what is necessary to maximize their long-term value and your company's profits.

To get there, though, you'll have to utterly transform not only the culture of your company, but the very the structures and functionalities that make your company work. Which leads us to the second challenge presented by customer centricity.

The Financial Challenge

This must be said: customer centricity will cost you money, at least in the short term. No change comes without challenge, of course, and although the long-term rewards of customer centricity may be clear, any company that undergoes a strategic change of this magnitude is surely going to take a short-term hit. Immediately after the adoption of a customer-centric model, your organization will have to be retooled to attain customer-centric success. You'll have to invest in the technologies and human capital necessary to collect and sort through data about your customers. You'll have to reorganize your organization to be more nimble, more flexible, and more responsive to the needs of your core customers. Essentially, you'll have to be willing to suffer a short-term loss in order to achieve a long-term gain. You may not hit your quarterly numbers; indeed, you may not hit your annual numbers. It may well take a long time to recoup the money you spend to make your firm customer centric because, as I've tried to stress here, the leap from product centricity to customer centricity is a fairly dramatic leap indeed.

So the question now is obvious. Given all the risk, given all the work required, and given the time and money that must be invested, why should you even bother? Well, simply because in many cases the rewards of customer centricity are simply too great. Yes, product centricity works. But for many companies and in many industries, customer centricity will work *better*.

In the last chapter, we examined the "virtuous cycle" that lies at the heart of product centricity—that wonderfully old-school, tried-and-true, simple business cycle that allows product-centric companies to realize cost savings (and by extension, profits) through increased productivity. It's effective and as a result, attractive to a great many businesses and executives.

But customer centricity delivers profits too. It's just that customer centricity delivers those profits in a slightly less cyclical, slightly more complicated, and (most important) slightly more sustainable fashion. Those long-term profits are realized because customer centricity allows companies to excel in three key areas:

1. Customer acquisition. Customer centricity can allow your company to better understand the true cost (and value) of new customer acquisition, help you better understand where your company should look for new customers, and can increase the number and quality of referrals from your existing customers— thereby helping you gather even more highly committed customers moving forward.

2. Customer retention. Customer centricity can lengthen the relationship between you and your best customers and allow you to maintain these relationships at lower cost.

3. Customer development. Customer centricity can boost the frequency with which your customers purchase a particular product or service from you, allow you to sell more varied products to your customers via cross-selling, allow you to realize a price premium from your best customers for an existing product or service, and allow you to up-sell your best customers to higher margin products or services.

None of these dynamics can be achieved easily, and there's certainly no guarantee that you'll achieve all of them at once (or *ever* achieve all of them, for that matter). But I'm guessing most companies would be thrilled to accomplish *any* of these goals—and if it is possible to achieve even three or four of the sub-goals previously mentioned on a regular basis, then the move toward customer centricity may be justified. Should you put a customer-centric infrastructure into place at your company, and should you commit yourself to the principles of this new model for business success, I believe you *will* enjoy some success. Maybe not immediate success. Maybe not earthshaking success. But success nonetheless—substantial, lasting success.

I am not here to tell you that customer centricity will solve all of your problems. I am not here to say that customer centricity can turn a bad company into a good company. And as you will learn in the chapters to come, I am not even saying that customer centricity is the right strategy for every single company in the world today—because it's not. I am saying, however, that when applied correctly, in the right circumstances, and with the right timeframe and expectations, customer centricity will make a difference—if not today, then certainly tomorrow, and for many years going forward.

Customer centricity can allow your organization to make far more money from your most valuable customers who will buy from you more often and spend more when they do buy from you. Customer centricity can help you create a passionate, committed customer base that will spread word of your company's attributes to potential new customers. Customer centricity can improve the way your customers view you—even as those customers pour more money into your coffers.

But most important, it will also generate profits—for the long term.

Few companies in the world understand this better than UK retailing giant Tesco. One of the true pioneers of the customer-centric mindset, Tesco continues to be viewed as one of the leaders in customer-centric thought today. And deservedly so; this company may not have invented customer centricity, but it certainly has gone a long way toward perfecting it.

Through its massively successful and ever-expanding Clubcard customer loyalty program, first introduced in 1995, Tesco has over the past two decades aimed to both better understand on the macro-level scale what kind of marketing initiatives and promotions and sales are working on a company-wide basis and also drill down to the micro-level scale to every individual customer and initiate company-customer interactions that make each and every one of those customers feel valued—and in the process, generate value back to the company.

Entire books have been written about Tesco's customer-centric initiatives, but really, the details of the program are quite simple. Every time a Clubcard patron buys something at Tesco, those patrons get points that are paid back to them four times per year and can be used, of course, to buy more Tesco products. So the customer wins. But Tesco wins too. It wins with data.

With each transaction made under the Clubcard program, Tesco gathers data about what was purchased, how much was spent, where the purchases were made, and more. In other words, through the Clubcard program, Tesco collects *knowledge* about each of its millions of customers—knowledge it can use (and does use, with enormous success) to target individual customers with offers, deals, or specials specifically customized to their wants, needs, and habits. On a larger scale, the company also uses that data to determine what kinds of stores to build in different markets and even how individual stores should be laid out.

Countless other retailers have similar initiatives, but few have approached their customer loyalty efforts with the sheer commitment Tesco has shown. Indeed, in their book *Scoring Points: How Tesco Is Winning Customer Loyalty*, Terry Hunt, Tim Phillips, and Clive Humby (one of the key figures behind the construction of the Clubcard program) write that the customer data collected through the Clubcard initiative guide many of the key business decisions made by Tesco executives.

It's a bold statement, but Tesco execs have reason to trust their data. Before the introduction of the Clubcard program, Tesco was the second-largest retailer in Britain. Today, thanks in large part to the customer-centric ideas at the heart of the company's customer loyalty program, Tesco is ranked first in its home market and third in the world, with more 4,800 locations around the globe and annual revenues of $62 billion as of 2010. And although in the past half decade Walmart has launched a campaign to beat Tesco in its core markets, the customer-centric UK titan has more than held its ground; in fact, in early 2011, London-based General Dynamics released a report predicting that Tesco would grow at an annual rate of 7.5% per year through 2015. That was the highest rate in the entire retail sector—higher even than that predicted for Walmart.

The Paradox of Customer Centricity: What about Your Other Customers?

As we've just learned, the basics of customer centricity are to identify, research, serve, and profit from the most valuable customers your company has—what we call the "right" customers. It is a simple idea that, admittedly, is not so simple to implement. And that's because the adoption of customer centricity demands nothing less than a complete restructuring of your organization that will position it to serve precisely the right customers at the expense of pretty much everything else. Now, understandably, many find this laser focus on a select few customers unsettling, and even for those who eventually come around to seeing the potential value in customer centricity, there often remains one big lingering question: what about all of the other customers? It's the elephant in the room. It is, as I like to call it, the paradox of customer centricity.

Let's take a step back for a moment. Imagine that your company has just decided to adopt customer centricity as its new organizational model. As soon as that decision was made, you and your colleagues would go about the work of reconfiguring your presumably product-centric company to fit within the customer-centric model. Product teams would be eliminated in favor of customer segment teams. Research and development processes would be broken down and rebuilt.

New metrics would be rolled out to measure organizational success. Employee rewards programs would be revamped to reflect customer-centric goals.

In other words, every single aspect of the organization would be reconfigured to serve those oh-so-desirable select customers: the right customers. It would be a radical shift indeed. But once you had gotten to this point—once you were ready to embark on your customer-centric future—I am guessing you or somebody else at your firm might ask that most obvious question: what about everybody else?

When I teach customer centricity, it doesn't take long for my students to begin asking that very question or some version of it. "If we are to concern ourselves only with the *right* customers," they ask, "what exactly are we supposed to do with the *rest* of the customers? Should be ignore them? Push them away? *Fire them*?"

The answer to all of those questions, of course, is no. Because even though I've spent nearly 10,000 words telling you all of the reasons why the product-centric model is old and dangerously vulnerable to a changing global marketplace, I will now admit that even if you create the most thoroughly customer-centric company that has ever existed, you will still need to be product-centric in a significant way.

Confused? Don't be. There's a logical explanation. As I've already explained, making the transition to customer centricity can be costly. Such a dramatic cultural and organization change will demand enormous amounts of time and effort. It will also require a huge infusion of money at the outset of the process and periodic infusions of money on an ongoing basis to keep the customer-centric ball rolling as you reorganize your company.

In order to do customer centricity right, you need to know almost everything there is to know about your customers, and knowing everything there is to know about your customer requires resources—people, technology, man-hours. It's a big mountain to climb. In the long term, of course, I believe these huge efforts—this massive expenditure of time and money—can and will pay equally huge dividends. But in the short term, well, there is the simple reality of paying the bills, making payroll, and staying in business.

This is where your other customers come in. It's also where we acknowledge the paradox of customer centricity. In a customer-centric company, as we spend more and more of our time and money focusing specifically on the right customers, it turns out that we actually need those other customers quite a bit. Indeed, it is very unlikely that we can survive without them.

It's not that difficult to figure out why. At the end of the day, your company—any company, really—will have a lot more other customers than right customers. And you know what? That's perfectly fine. Desirable, even. Because simple math dictates that, at least in the short term, those much more numerous other customers are probably going to generate more profits (collectively, not individually) than the right customers. This is especially true—and here is a key point—if you don't actually have to put much effort into making those profits happen.

Yes, you want those other customers to stick around. You want them to buy your products and services. You want them to provide the steady influx of cash that will allow you to continue your work toward capitalizing on the right customers. You want these other customers to keep right on being your customers; you just don't want to burn any calories worrying about them. What I'm suggesting here is that you should view these other customers as low-hanging fruit. They are easy money. They are, in essence, the ballast that will allow you to continue on your path to long-term customer-centric success. In that sense, they remain every bit as important to your company as the right customers.

And while those right customers get your best efforts, the others don't. And no, there's nothing wrong with that. From a strictly business perspective, in fact, it's the right way to do things.

I always stress to my students that the decision to become a customer-centric company is most certainly not a decision to become a boutique company.

We in the customer-centric world are not downsizers. We don't want to shrink our customer pool or limit profits. Rather, we are simply interested in allocating our resources in the most efficient way possible. Again, let us remember the point on which we began this chapter: the goal of a customer-centric firm is precisely the same goal of a product-centric firm. The goal is to make money—lots of money—for the long term. To generate enormous profits. To grow. To create shareholder value.

It just so happens that, in order to do these things, we in the customer-centric world need the very customers whom we can openly say we don't necessarily spend any time thinking about. They are, in essence, like cash in an investment portfolio. They offer balance, scale, safety, stability. That's why we can't slam the door in their faces. That's why we can't—and don't—turn our backs on them.

Which brings me to my last point.

Now that we've established that customer-centric companies actually do need those other customers—the ones we're barely going to pay attention to—it certainly would be fair to ask whether there is something inherently *hypocritical* about customer centricity. But I assure you, customer centricity is *not* hypocritical.

Although we in the customer-centric world continue to keep the doors open to those other customers, and although we certainly want those customers to keep buying *our* products instead of our competitors' products, we also understand on a very fundamental level the cost-benefit ratio that forms the basis of our relationship with those other customers. We want those other customers to keep coming back, so long as they don't cause any trouble, don't waste our time, and don't cost us a single cent more than it takes for us to keep them coming back. We customer-centric types acknowledge that we are better off spending our time worrying about the right customers, not whether one of the other customers stays or goes. *That* is why customer centricity is different than product centricity.

In our world, we don't believe (as Nordstrom apparently believes) that all customers are created equal. We don't believe the customer is always right. We don't bend over backward to make each and every customer happy. And we certainly don't kowtow to customers who try to return a set of used tires that we didn't sell in the first place. Yes, we need the other customers as a collective asset, even though any one of them is quite expendable. But we live or die based on the right customers—and want to invest heavily to find and serve more like them.

In the next chapter, I'll explain why.

Chapter 3

Customer Equity: New Views on Value

In this chapter:

- What is brand equity?
- What is customer equity?
- What kinds of companies are more likely to find value in customer equity?

What Is Brand Equity?

As we've already established, the aim for any company—product centric, customer centric, or somewhere in between—is to make the most money possible and generate the greatest profits possible, with the ultimate goal of maximizing the value of the company and bolstering shareholder equity.

The first question we need to tackle is this: where does that equity—that total value—actually come from?

It's a simple question that would seem to have rather a simple answer. And it does—depending on whom you ask. Talk to a traditionalist or somebody with a more practical view of business and you'll likely hear that a firm's total equity can be derived by adding up all of the assets, tangible and otherwise, that can be found in one of two equity silos. There is, of course, financial equity, which includes such basics as cash, real estate, investments in other firms, and other financial assets. And then there is operational equity, which encompasses a company's technologies, product lines, human capital, and more. Add the two together and there you have it: a company's total equity.

It's hard to argue with this methodology, of course. It's simple, straightforward, and grounded in the world of the tangible. But as it turns out, determining a company's total equity is a tad more complicated than this two-pronged approach might suggest. Indeed, an increasing number of academics and other forward-thinking business minds are starting to agree that the task of quantifying a company's total equity requires some more thorough and more creative thinking (not to mention a little bit of guesswork) about what, exactly, qualifies as equity in the first place. In fact, these people would have you believe that equity can also be found in two additional silos.

The more widely accepted of these two equity silos—and the one you've more than likely come across by now—is brand equity, a rather novel and still-controversial idea that nonetheless can be traced directly to the staid world of product centricity, where brand managers reign supreme. According to the brand equity backers, companies can find real, quantifiable value in their brands and in their brand portfolios. In other words, proponents of brand equity believe that, just as Coca-Cola could (and would) count its Atlanta headquarters building as an asset, so too could (and should) the company count its flagship Coke *brand* as an asset. The premise here, very simply, is that a company's logo, its reputation, and even its name have actual financial value. Some of the bolder brand-equity backers would even argue that the value of a truly great brand could actually be greater than the value of all of that company's other assets *combined*.

At first blush, that may seem to be a fairly radical statement. But again, I would ask you to look at Coca-Cola. Think about that company long and hard enough, and I think you might agree with the assessment made by many branding experts that the Coke *brand*—the signature script logo of classic Coca-Cola, the sleek sliver can of Diet Coke (which, it should be noted, recently surpassed Pepsi as the world's second most popular soda behind regular Coke)—actually *is* more valuable than everything else Coke owns. That's the absolute dream of a brand-oriented company. So why not formally assign it a value and carry it as an asset on the balance sheet?

It should be noted that this line of thought is hardly limited to the world of academia or folks such as myself. In fact, in some more civilized nations, companies can and do actually list their brands as assets on their balance sheets. This is the case in the United Kingdom. It's also the case in Australia. And really, it's not hard to see why. Although we haven't yet developed the math that can tell us *exactly* how to calculate brand equity, it's certainly obvious that there is enormous value in a powerhouse brand.

It's an interesting argument, and not one that I'll dismiss. But although brand equity may indeed be real, and it may one day be quantifiable in a manner that CPAs around the world will accept, I'm fairly certain that it's often not quite as important or as valuable to a company's overall equity as is the last piece of our equity puzzle, customer equity.

What Is Customer Equity?

Much like customer centricity as a whole, the notion of customer equity remains somewhat on the fringes of business practices today, so I'm quite certain there is far greater backing for the formalization of brand equity than there is for the widespread introduction of customer equity to mainstream marketing discussion or even balance sheets. With that said, I'm hopeful.

I'm hopeful because I see progress being made and because I can actually foresee a day (in the not-too-distant future, actually) when the math on which customer equity is built will actually be solid enough to win over both the holdouts in my own field of marketing and the good people of the finance world as well. Even today, in fact, my sense is that those finance folks—the CFOs, the accountants, the auditors—are already more comfortable with the ideas behind customer equity than they are with those ideas behind brand equity. They appear willing to believe that a customer might actually be a more appropriate fit on a balance sheet than a nebulous brand could ever be. They are starting to see, I think, that when it comes to customers—those miniature profit centers that power *every* company's growth—there is some real value there. You know what? They're right.

As a believer in the ideas behind customer equity, I am generally pleased when anyone even makes a passing mention of the idea. I believe in these ideas, after all, so I want them out there. But it bothers me when people talk about customer equity as some kind of hazy, indefinable concept because customer equity is *anything but* hazy or indefinable. It really can be quantified (although, I admit, not always as precisely as we might hope); it can (and should) be counted among a company's assets; and most important, it can be leveraged to generate future growth.

Customer equity, quite simply, lies at the very heart of customer centricity. We can't become customer centric until we understand customer equity—what it

is, how we define it, and what we're supposed to do
with it.

I define it as follows:

*Customer equity is the sum of the customer lifetime
values across a firm's entire customer base.*

The implications of this straightforward definition are fairly obvious. If we are to agree (and I think
we do) that every company's objective is to maximize its overall equity, and if we agree (and I think we
do) that customer equity can and should be counted
toward a company's overall equity, then we must also
agree that companies should dedicate the resources
necessary to do whatever it takes to *maximize* that
customer equity.

Of course, before we can maximize customer
equity—and before we can begin to evaluate our
success in doing so—we must know how to *quantify*
customer equity. And as my definition suggests, we
can't do that until we know the value—the customer
lifetime value (CLV)—of each and every one of our
customers. There are quite a few different models and
equations out there that claim to be able to do precisely this. Some are mostly correct, some are a little
bit correct, and some are wildly off the mark, but all
of these various formulas agree on the point we've
already touched on: a company's total customer

equity is calculated by adding up the CLV of all its individual customers.

Sounds simple, right? Unfortunately, it's not. In fact, it's a great deal more complicated than some academics and industry insiders have recently made it sound.

Which Companies Are More Likely to Find Value in Customer Equity?

In the next chapter, we'll begin to dig deeper into the quantification of customer equity—how it has traditionally been quantified, how it *should* be quantified, and how it can and has been put to use in the real world. But I feel compelled to first reiterate that although I am obviously a proponent of customer centricity, and although I do believe this new model for success holds enormous value for companies in today's volatile and competitive marketplace, I also realize that customer centricity makes more sense for some companies than it does for others.

So before we go any further, we should establish whether customer equity is something your company should fully commit itself to acquiring. To answer that question, we need to first explore two *other* questions that, in a sense, draw an ever-important and, in some cases, very real line between those firms that naturally lend themselves to a product-centric approach and those that may be better suited to a customer-centric approach.

1. What kinds of firms are more likely to grow via brand equity?

2. What kinds of firms are more likely to grow via customer equity?

I often pose these questions to executives, managers, and other front-line practitioners through my work with Wharton Executive Education, not to mention my students in the Wharton MBA program. In the years I've put them out for discussion, I've been impressed, confused, surprised, and sometimes downright perplexed by the responses I've received. While the answers often make clear that customer centricity can often be a difficult topic to tackle, they also generate great discussion, foster interesting insights—and most notably, reinforce my belief that for some companies, it is *absolutely inexcusable* not to be moving forward in a customer-centric manner.

And for others? Well, for others, product centricity might actually be the safest course of action.

The answers to the first question are generally both predictable and absolutely on target, as product-centric powerhouse as Coca-Cola and Apple are overwhelmingly tabbed as companies that could rightly claim enormous brand equity as a major source of value and a principal asset for future growth. As we've already discussed, both of these highly successful firms live firmly in the product-centric world. They thrive in a product-centric world. They are powered by brand and product. They may *value* their customers, but it's unclear whether they really care about those customers' *values*. And to be honest, it's hard to blame them. They're doing just fine.

As for that second question? Well, the answers are decidedly more muddled. In many discussions over the years, I've heard cable giant Comcast named as a potentially customer-equity-rich firm. Not a bad answer. American Express (a good choice) and American Airlines (also a good choice) have been selected as well. Universities have been said to hold great customer-equity potential (possibly). And of course, so has Apple—which as you might imagine has caused me no small amount of consternation. In other words, when it comes to identifying potentially customer-equity-rich firms, there is hardly a consensus, either in the real world or in academia.

I find the general confusion downright unsurprising. Again, customer centricity operates on the fringe, and as a result, there just aren't many obvious icons of customer centricity out there today; we certainly don't yet have an Apple of customer centricity. There just isn't a firm that has perfected this art to the point where it is a paragon for all others. At least not yet. Tesco is an excellent candidate for this honor, but its name doesn't come up very often. Maybe Amazon. But neither of them has the same global visibility for their customer-centric efforts as Coca-Cola and Apple have for their brands.

Which brings me to my point. Although even experts in the field have yet to come to consensus on the standout customer-equity-rich firm, there is a general agreement on the vast *potential* of customer equity for certain markets and certain industries; by extension, there is also some agreement that some markets still exist in which customer centricity might not actually be of much use.

Among those insights—which I agree with, it should be noted—are the following:

- Contractual firms (e.g., those that utilize subscription models, such as Comcast, a health club, or a performing arts organization) are more likely to find value in customer equity; noncontractual firms will tend toward brand equity.

- Companies that sell highly customized offerings (e.g., investment advisors and grocery stores, in which every customer's portfolio or cart full of items looks very different) are more likely to find value in customer equity; companies that sell non-customizable, commoditized offerings (e.g., ice-cream stores and laser eye surgeons) should focus more on brand equity.

■ Companies that sell highly visible products—think sneakers or high-end clothing—are more likely to find value in brand equity.

■ Companies that have powerful intermediaries standing between them and their end users (e.g., a consumer packaged-good manufacturer, a publisher, or a pharmaceutical firm) are more likely to find value in brand equity.

■ Companies that inherently establish long-term relationships with their customers (e.g., insurance companies and educational institutions) are more likely to find value in customer equity.

■ Companies that sell services are more generally likely to find value in customer equity than product-oriented firms.

■ Companies that can't easily obtain customer-level data (for technological or regulatory reasons) are more inclined to focus on brand equity.

Of course, none of these criteria are hard-and-fast dividing lines, and the list is far from complete, but I find this thought exercise to be an excellent one to better understand the distinctions between brand equity and customer equity—and thus product centricity or customer centricity. In other words—and I emphasize this point because it's important—some firms and some markets simply lend themselves more easily to the idea of customer equity, and customer centricity in general, than others. I believe it is quite valuable to carefully think about relevant criteria like these and what they can tell us about a company's suggested strategy.

But at the same time, other criteria may seem to be diagnostic but really aren't. For instance, looking back on my discussions with customer-centric thinkers over the years, I recall some suggesting that new companies would naturally tend toward customer equity (but how about Groupon as a striking counterexample), whereas others said very mature companies would do the same (to which I offer this: *Coca-Cola*). There are a number of other nondiagnostic criteria, such as high versus low product/service involvement (chewing gum should lean toward brand equity, but your local water utility should lean toward customer equity) and health-oriented products/services (Johnson & Johnson plays the brand card, while your primary care physician ought to be customer focused). Notice that in both of these examples, the service versus product distinction swamps the other criteria.

Try thinking of a few other criteria and examples of firms associated with them. This exercise will really help you appreciate the key concepts I'm trying to convey here.

But what does this all mean? It means that nothing about customer centricity is cut-and-dried. A single approach won't work in all business settings. For some firms, an orientation toward customer centricity will prove to be enormously useful. For others, it will be somewhat useful. And for still others, well, it may be a poor use of their resources. But all firms should give it serious consideration and think very carefully about it as a strategic option. Just because this option is risky or unfamiliar is not enough reason to reject it.

If you conclude that customer equity is something you want, and if you decide that you really do want to know what your customers are *really* worth, then read on. In the next chapter, I'll explain how you gain precisely that knowledge—and start taking meaningful steps toward customer-centric success.

Chapter 4

Customer Lifetime Value: The Real Worth of Your Customers

In this chapter:

- What is customer lifetime value (CLV)?
- What can CLV do for your company?
- Why are traditional approaches to CLV calculations flawed?
- How can customer segmentation create more accurate CLV calculations?

What Is Customer Lifetime Value?

In the last chapter we looked at the basics of customer equity, explored how it contrasts with the more established notion of brand equity, and examined the kinds of companies that might be most interested in building customer equity.

In this chapter, we are going to discuss one of the bedrock ideas behind customer centricity: customer lifetime value (CLV). Our discussions here—both about what CLV is and how it should be calculated—

will help you better and more accurately assess the value of your customers. By extension, this will allow you to run your company more intelligently and more efficiently than ever before.

CLV is the very unit of measurement upon which customer centricity and customer-centric firms are built. CLV is the unit of measurement that creates customer equity, which in turn creates greater firm value. CLV helps us value our customers individually and collectively, establishes an upper bound on what we should be willing to spend to acquire new customers, and enables us to make better decisions about the allocation of marketing resources across the customer base.

I define CLV as follows:

Customer lifetime value is the present value of the future (net) cash flows associated with a particular customer.

This may seem to be a fairly simple and straightforward definition. But as with many other elements of customer centricity, there is some nuance here—as well as a good bit of confusion out there in the real world regarding what CLV is and what it isn't.

Therefore, before we take a look at how CLV has traditionally been calculated, and how a simple customer-centric tweak can improve upon that traditional method, I should first clarify four key points.

1. CLV is a forward-looking concept. CLV should not be confused with a customer's past profitability. When we calculate CLV, we are not looking backward. We are not concerned with how much value Joe Smith brought to us over the past year (there's another term for that: profit). What we are most concerned with (and rightly so) is how much Joe Smith is going to be worth *tomorrow*. And next week. And next month. And next year. In other words, we are interested in finding out how much money Joe Smith could potentially make for our company from now until eternity, and therefore, how much money we should be willing to spend to keep him. In a sense, this is what CLV gives us.

Unfortunately, countless companies and even many academics make the mistake of viewing past profitability as being the same as CLV or, at the very least, as being very tightly related to CLV. Yes, there is some correlation here. Yes, past profitability can offer you some *indication* of what a customer might be worth in the future. And yes, it can offer you a hint of how a customer *might* act in the future. But it is not CLV. They are different concepts entirely. It's crucial to keep that in mind.

2. It is essential to use only relevant data to calculate CLV. For instance, although a proper calculation of CLV must take into account customer acquisition costs, *only* the most directly applicable of those costs should be considered. Some would propose that companies should consider *all* marketing and advertising dollars when calculating CLV; I happen to disagree. To my way of thinking, only those dollars *specifically* associated with a *specific* customer should be considered when running these calculations. To do otherwise would potentially skew the results and sabotage your CLV efforts.

3. CLV calculations are predictive, not precise. Even if you were to access every data point you desired about customer Joe Smith, and even if you scrubbed that data to ensure pinpoint accuracy, you still wouldn't necessarily arrive at a truly accurate, truly actionable CLV for customer Joe Smith. Although the textbook formula seems to suggest that you can get a precise and true and accurate CLV—for example, that Joe Smith's CLV is $1,500,000—it is actually making a *prediction* for Joe Smith's CLV. We are making a guess— an educated guess, but a guess nonetheless. This must always be acknowledged. There is plenty of variability involved in that guess, and we should never forget it.

4. Different methods are used to calculate CLV in different kinds of business settings. In the previous chapter, I pointed out the important distinction between a contractual and a noncontractual relationship—and this distinction carries all the way through the mathematical calculations associated with CLV. As one example, the terms "retention" and "churn" apply specifically and exclusively to the contractual setting: will we continue to hold this customer's business when he decides whether or not to renew his contract? But these words make no sense at all in the noncontractual domain. Noncontractual firms (ranging from Amazon to your dentist to a car dealer) should rightfully obsess over repeat purchases, but this is an entirely different concept than retention. If a customer buys from your company one time and another noncontractual vendor next time, that doesn't mean your company has undergone churn, as it would if that customer drops his or her subscription with your contractual firm.

So with these complications (among many others) in mind, we acknowledge that CLV calculations have their limits. Customer centricity has its limits too. And this is why I believe the naïve thinkers—those who believe their CLV calculations are creating a pinpoint value—are wrong. If we are being completely honest, we will admit that when we calculate CLV we're actually creating an *expectation* of value.

You may think I'm quibbling here, but this a very important distinction to make because far too many companies have run CLV numbers and leapt to the conclusion that the numbers generated are "the" numbers that will guarantee customer-centric success. They then spend a ton of money to build a system for customer relationship management and expect it to solve all of their problems. As you'll learn in the next chapter, that is simply not how it works.

What Can CLV Do for Your Company?

When we calculate CLV we want to find a data point that we can actually put to use at our companies with confidence. But this doesn't always come easily.

As we have already established, customer-centric firms are committed to creating processes, products, and services specifically geared toward the needs, demands, and projected future whims of their most committed customers, all with the ultimate aim of maximizing the profit of each and every one. To do this, however, these companies need good, solid, actionable data, and CLV—the expected lifetime value of a customer—is the most important data they can have because it gives companies a greater understanding of what their customers (as individuals and as a group) are actually worth; by extension, CLV helps those companies more clearly understand which customers are the right customers and which customers are just along for the ride.

When calculated correctly, CLV can

- tell you what your individual customer is worth;

- allow you to estimate the value of your company's overall customer equity;

- enable your company to divide customers into tangible segments, separating the most valuable and committed customers into different groups and distinguishing them from the less valuable but numerous others;

- create opportunities to help you refine marketing practices and ensure that the right approaches are being made to the right customers;

- allow you to better predict how certain customers in certain situations might act going forward; and

- ensure that resources are used more efficiently in efforts to retain and develop existing customers and acquire new ones.

CLV, quite simply, can be enormously important information. But its importance is directly linked to its accuracy—and unfortunately, most companies today are calculating their CLV in a flawed manner. As it turns out, the reason is that the most widely accepted methods for calculating CLV are flawed as well.

Why Are Traditional Approaches to CLV Calculations Flawed?

These methods are flawed because they violate the cardinal rule of customer centricity. They do not acknowledge (much less *celebrate*) the undeniable reality of customer heterogeneity. These traditional methods were created with the purpose of giving companies the precise CLV of "the customer." In this sense, they assume that, given a certain amount of information (for example, average customer retention rate, discount rate, net cash flow per period, and so on), a marketing manager can simply run some calculations and arrive at "the" CLV for any particular customer at any particular point in time. To this way of thinking, new customers should be treated the same as customers who have been around for years, and it assumes that Customer A will act the same way as Customer B.

For example, some companies might believe that all they need to do in order to calculate their overall customer equity is to take look at *all* of their existing customers as one massive homogenous group, calculate the CLV for "the average customer," then multiply by the size of the customer base. This approach is simple, straightforward, and easily accomplished. It's also completely wrong.

If we are to accept that different customers will act in different ways, then we simply cannot accept the idea that the value of all of those customers—the CLV of each individual and the collective customer equity of all of those individuals put together—can be derived from the same set of data calculated in the same way, no matter their circumstances, their inherent levels of loyalty, their commitment to our firms, or their overall tenure as customers.

These traditional methods for calculating CLV were conceived with good intentions—that is, to help customer-centric firms make more educated customer-centric decisions. Unfortunately, these methods fall short, for the simple reason that they have not been implemented in a customer-centric manner.

In other words, I would argue that CLV can only prove valuable if it remains true at all times to customer-centric principles.

How Can Customer Segmentation Create More Accurate CLV Calculations?

There is no one-size-fits-all solution in CLV, just as there is no one-size-fits-all solution in customer centricity. The most fundamental flaw of traditional methods for calculating CLV (and by extension, customer equity) is the idea that one formula can be applied to all customers and give companies a clear idea of what their customers are worth. This flaw becomes readily apparent if we look at even just one key data point in any CLV calculation: retention rate.

Although we will not dive deeply into the math of CLV in this book, I believe the examples that follow— one hypothetical, the other from the real world—will make clear just how important it can be to treat different kinds of customers in different ways when calculating CLV. They will also reveal how the simple act of customer segmentation can give you a clearer sense of your company's overall customer equity. For the purposes of this book, it is not really important for you to understand the formulas at the heart of CLV; instead, I want you to walk away with an understanding of the pitfalls other companies have faced when trying to put CLV to use—and how some bedrock customer-centric ideas can improve upon the traditional methods for helping companies better understand the behaviors and value of their customer base.

Let's start with the hypothetical.

According to traditional CLV calculations, all customers in a contractual business setting (for example, subscribers to a magazine) essentially carry with them a "retention coin." For each retention period, those customers flip that coin. If that coin comes up heads, the customer stays; if it comes up tails, they leave. So the probability of a customer staying for four time periods, for example, could be represented quite simply as the probability of a customer's coin coming up heads four times in a row. Such math would create a very specifically shaped survival curve that in theory illustrates how many customers will still be around after four years. That survival curve is essentially a slow, consistent decline, as illustrated in figure 1.

The math that created this curve seems reasonable enough. But the reality is that such a curve is almost *never* borne out by the data. A true survival curve, as it turns out, does not gently decline in a steady manner. Rather, these real-world curves show a rather dramatic drop early on—and then a rather surprising leveling off, as illustrated in figure 2.

The lesson here is twofold. Not only is the traditional method the wrong way to value our customers (as you'll soon see, this formula actually *undervalues* customers), it also tells us the wrong story about customer behavior. That second curve, however, tells us the right story. It's a story we can arrive at through a simple tweak to the textbook formula—a tweak based on segmentation. It is an idea that plays directly into the core beliefs of customer centricity and, according to my way of thinking, markedly improves upon the traditional methods of calculating CLV and customer equity.

Figure 1: Textbook Survival Curve

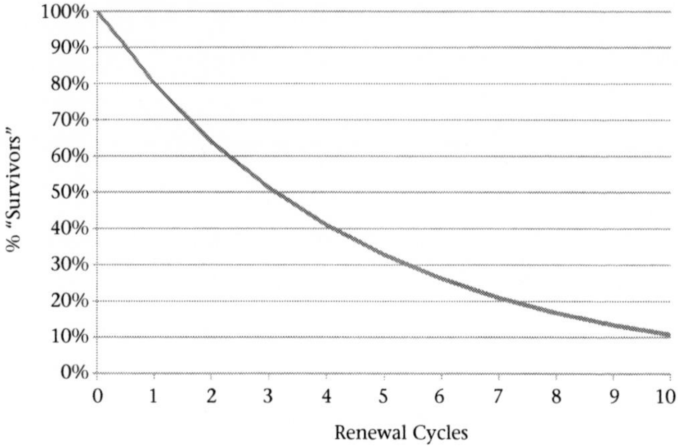

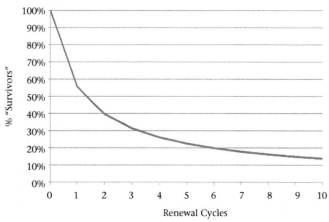

Figure 2: Real-World Survival Curve

Through segmentation, we acknowledge that some customers will have very tails-prone retention coins, which means they will leave us very early in our relationship. Others are much more heads-prone, which we could possible attribute to loyalty or just inertia. But here's the key: when those tails-prone customers start to drop off in the first few periods, we are left with a much more homogeneous group that largely consists of fairly heads-prone customers. This is why the survival curve drops quickly, then levels off.

In other words, the retention dynamics that we tend to see in a contractual setting have little or nothing to do with customers becoming more loyal over time (unlike the conventional wisdom that virtually every company on Earth subscribes to). These retention dynamics are primarily due to the shake-out that occurs as the customer base undergoes a natural form of self-selection. This has enormous implications for CLV calculations and for allocating resources across customers.

For example, many contractual companies essentially bribe their customers to stick around, in the hope that they will become more loyal over time; think about the stories you've heard from customers who extract goodies from a cable company or mobile provider when they threaten to leave at the end of a contract. I generally think this is a very bad idea for most companies—especially when it comes to "ordinary" customers. Instead, they should simply count on the natural selection process to weed out the good from the bad and spend their resources finding more new customers who resemble the good ones. This is a major departure from conventional thinking about customer valuation (and customer centricity in general), but it is an important lesson that should not be overlooked.

Now let's turn to our second example, which shows the implications of accounting for heterogeneity in a real-world setting. Vodafone Italia, the mobile powerhouse that recorded revenues of more than $2 billion in 2010, is one of the companies that has taken the first crucial step toward a clearer, more accurate picture of the value of its customer base. The company has taken that step through the smart and completely commonsense use of customer churn segmentation as illustrated in figure 3.

Unlike some of its competitors, Vodafone is smart enough to understand that not all of its customers will renew their subscriptions with the same frequency. Some are more likely to renew, and others are significantly less likely to renew. As a result, when working to understand its overall customer equity, the company doesn't just look at the average renewal rate of all of its customers; instead, it breaks those customers down into three customer segments, each grouped by their propensity to renew. This segmentation may on its face seem to do little to change the average renewal rate, the expected lifetime of a customer, or a predictive CLV. But as it turns out, the difference is a fairly significant one—and quite illustrative, I think, of how segmenting customers can paint a much truer picture of the value of your customer base.

Figure 3: Churn Segments for Vodafone Italia

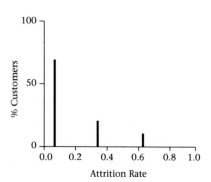

Cluster	Attrition Rate	% customers
Low risk	0.06	70
Medium risk	0.35	20
High risk	0.65	10

Source: "Vodafone Achievement and Challenges in Italy" presentation (September 12, 2003)

A few years back, when the company first began its use of churn segmentation, it broke its customer base into three cohorts, as the illustration shows. As you can see, if Vodafone had employed a nonsegmented approach to calculate the expected lifetime of its customers—if it had simply taken the average churn rate across all of its customers and plugged into conventional formulas—it would have come up with an average churn rate of 17.7%:

$0.06 \times 0.70 + 0.35 \times 0.20 + 0.65 \times 0.10 = 0.177$ (or 17.7%)

A churn rate of 17.7% should lead to an expected lifetime of 5.6 years:

$1/0.177 = 5.6$ years

That would be the usual textbook approach—which represents the state-of-the-art valuation methodology for consultants and investment banks that help firms value their customer base for mergers and acquisition purposes.

Now let's do it the *right* way—explicitly taking heterogeneity into account. For each segment, we will calculate expected lifetime in the same way (i.e., 1/churn), but *we'll take the average afterward*. This gives us an expected lifetime of 12.4 years:

$(16.7 \times 0.70) + (2.9 \times 0.20) + (1.5 \times 0.10) = 12.4$ years

The customer base is suddenly worth more than twice as much simply by doing the calculation correctly. How about that! I'm sure you agree this is a huge difference. And think about the implications for investment professionals who would be undervaluing customer equity (and thus the company as a whole) by more than 50%. (Of course, if you are on the buy side of mergers and acquisition activity, you might want to keep this quiet!) Through simple segmentation, firms like Vodaphone have been able to achieve a much truer picture of the value of their customer base. As a result, these firms are much better prepared to serve those customers—and capitalize upon those it expects to remain for years to come.

It should be noted that this Vodaphone example is no fluke; by no means was this example cherry-picked to overstate this point. Indeed, research has borne out a rather startling truth: when companies fail to apply segmentation to the study of their customer base, they will grossly *undervalue* that customer base. I have seen numerous other cases where the naïve approach to CLV leaves similar amounts of money on the table.

Which brings us back, once more, to the basics of customer centricity. If there's one point that I've attempted to make so far in this book, it is that companies simply cannot afford to hide behind the convenient myth of customer homogeneity. In the old days they didn't know any better because customer-level data were unavailable. But today that excuse is no longer valid—and the perils of ignoring heterogeneity are quite severe.

A Quick Discussion about Noncontractual Businesses

As noted earlier, terms like "retention" and "churn" don't apply in the noncontractual world. Customers do go away in the noncontractual setting, but they do so silently; they have no need to tell the firm they are leaving by walking away from a contractual relationship. This makes for a much trickier CLV calculation. We have to look at the time since a customer's last transaction and ask a question: is the customer alive but dormant, or is the customer "dead"? Some firms use simple rules of thumb to define an active customer from a "dead" one. For instance, Amazon uses a one-year hiatus to define a lapsed customer. But this definition is entirely arbitrary—and it can be quite dangerous. In many cases, firms will write off light-buying customers too prematurely. Maybe we don't care about any one of these customers; it is unlikely that they are the kinds of focal customers who deserve red-carpet treatment. But on the other hand, these light buyers can be a huge chunk of the customer base—the ballast that I referred to in chapter 2.

State-of-the-art CLV models capture this issue by focusing on the interplay between recency and frequency of each customer's transaction history. Along with monetary value (i.e., spend per transaction) the noncontractual firm has three key variables that should drive its CLV calculations. And although such models can indeed be fairly complex, the origins of the recency-frequency-monetary value rubric go back to Lester Wunderman and the other pioneers of direct marketing. (See my paper, "RFM and CLV: Using Iso-

Value Curves for Customer Base Analysis," published in the *Journal of Marketing Research* in November 2005 and available from my website, www.petefader.com.)

We've come full circle.

Thus, at every step in your journey toward customer-centric success, from adoption to implementation, you must always keep in mind the core principles we explored at the start of this book. "The customer" doesn't exist. You must not only accept but celebrate the idea of customer heterogeneity. By putting forth the effort to better understand the habits, tendencies, and *value* of each and every one of our customers, you can build better, stronger, and more profitable companies.

These ideas must be at the forefront as you work on the macro-level scale to retrofit your companies to compete in the post-product-centric world, and on the micro-level scale as you get down into the weeds of CLV, the very building block of customer equity, in the hope of refining as much as humanly possible our understanding of what your customers are really worth—and by extension, how far you should go to keep them, to please them, and to ensure their profitability for years and years to come.

Chapter 5

Customer Relationship Management: The First Step Toward Customer Centricity

In this chapter:

- How does customer relationship management (CRM) serve customer centricity?
- What is CRM—and what should it actually do?
- Why is CRM just the first step toward success in customer centricity?

How Does Customer Relationship Management (CRM) Serve Customer Centricity?

I need you to ignore, just for a moment, the fact that most companies of any decent size will indeed need a large and elaborate customer relationship management (CRM) system to succeed in bringing customer centricity to life. I need you to divert your attention from the big picture—bottom lines and retention rates and stock prices and long-term strategy—and think, just for a moment, about the one-to-one relationship between a business and a customer. I need you to step out of the corporate world and step onto Main Street because it's there, I think, that we can often find the best examples of CRM (and customer centricity) at work.

I want you to imagine a beauty salon on Main Street. The owner is a woman named Natasha, and she's been running her shop for years, providing her small town with all manner of services—hair styling, nails, facial treatments. Her customers include grandmothers and mothers and little girls—entire families, really—and she's long been the go-to beauty shop in town, surviving and even thriving in both good times and bad. At Natasha's, the customers keep coming back and sending their friends and family too. This means Natasha keeps making profits, quarter after quarter, year after year. Her business is not just stable. It is growing, even though the services she offers are really no better than the other salons in town.

How has Natasha pulled it off? Simple. In her own way, she built her beauty shop, her business, and her livelihood through customer centricity powered by CRM. She has thrived thanks to information and smart action on that information. Natasha's beauty shop is not only customer centricity exemplified, it's also an example of CRM perfected. And it's all in the cards—the big stack of index cards that help her to remember key details about key customers. She doesn't know everything about everyone—in fact, for many customers (the "others" that I've referred to in previous chapters), she doesn't make much effort at all. Of course, she is happy to work with new customers whom she has never met before, and they collectively make up a reasonable fraction of her volume and profits. But what makes Natasha so successful is her ability to leverage the data she has collected on her focal customers over the years.

Those index cards are Natasha's CRM. They are the memory chips on which she saves the crucial information that makes her special in the eyes of her customers: birthdays, anniversaries, names of kids, likes and dislikes, product preferences, spending limits, favorite vacation destinations, and long-term aspirations. Those cards, in other words, offer her the bits of information she might be able to use for profit in the future—to promote a manicure or pedicure, provide someone a special discount to celebrate a child's graduation, or even to suggest relevant products and services that aren't offered at her salon. These customer-centric recommendations help lock in clients for the long run, at least as effectively as the quality of the services themselves.

Natasha knows what her customers want. She knows what they need. She knows what they might be convinced to buy, given the right opportunity. She knows which customers can be developed into big spenders, as well as which ones will demand more of her time than they are worth. She knows what services she can't provide—and she knows the value of pointing her customers in another direction should they ask for what she can't deliver. She also knows that by sending her customers elsewhere, she isn't *losing* business, but rather winning loyalty that will ultimately create greater value in the long term.

Because she knows all of this, she is perfectly positioned to succeed on two fronts. She can succeed in the bottom-line sense, of course, but she can also succeed on a deeply *personal* level, leveraging her vast well of information to enable the establishment of connections between company and customer that even the mightiest of corporations would envy. Natasha has succeeded because she is more than just a hair stylist. She isn't just a service provider. She is a trusted advisor, somebody her customers will keep returning to year after year after year, simply because they actually believe Natasha has their best interests in mind.

Now, maybe she does or maybe she doesn't. But in the end, it's uncertain whether that actually matters. What matters, from a strictly bottom-line perspective, is that Natasha's efforts—her customer-centric efforts—*work*. And they work because Natasha really understands CRM—what it can do, what it can't do, and how it should be properly put to use to ensure customer-centric success. She also understands that the baseline functionality of her simple CRM system—the gathering of informal data—is merely the first step toward her customer-centric success, and that after the data have been gathered via CRM, the work has just begun.

Anybody can open a beauty salon. Any company can sell groceries. Any entrepreneur can invent a cool new technology. And any firm can purchase a fancy CRM system to collect mountains of data about their customers.

But that's not enough.

In the end, it's about the index cards—and not just buying the index cards, either. It's about the savvy to know what information about each customer to track on those cards, the genuine desire to care about the information on those cards, the ability to effectively use the information on those cards, and the persistence to continually update the information on those cards. It's about using those cards in the smartest, most strategic ways possible—and in so doing, giving your company an enormous advantage.

It sounds easy, but based on the common perceptions of—and frequent disappointment with—CRM, it's hard to replicate this example on a systematic, enterprise-wide basis.

What Is CRM—and What Should It Actually Do?

The story about Natasha the hairdresser is just that, a story. But the way Natasha practices CRM is the way that CRM really should be practiced, and the way Natasha uses CRM is the way CRM really should be used. Unfortunately, Natasha's pitch-perfect execution isn't all that common in the real world. CRM's reputation has suffered as a result. In this chapter, I'll explain why.

Before we go any further, though, I should step back and establish exactly what CRM is—or maybe more accurately, what it was *supposed* to be, before it got all messed up—and the crucially important role it plays within a broader customer-centric strategy.

A standard definition of CRM might read as follows:

CRM is a coordinated set of systems that a company uses to help create and extract more value from its customer base.

A more suitable definition of CRM—and the definition I prefer, actually—would be this:

A direct manifestation of the customer centricity business philosophy, CRM represents a firm's front-line efforts to gather data about and better understand the unique characteristics and expected value of its focal customers and to use that information to appropriately allocate resources.

CRM, quite simply, is customer centricity put into practice. And when implemented properly and used intelligently, CRM systems can be of tremendous use to any company aiming to become more customer centric.

More specifically, CRM enables companies to

- identify who their focal customers are (and aren't);

- more accurately estimate customer lifetime value (CLV) for individual customers and, by extension, to more accurately calculate overall customer equity;

- segment their customers into distinct groups to more efficiently and effectively execute subsequent marketing activities (acquisition, retention, and development);

- create the infrastructure to conduct this multistep process in a consistent manner on a regular basis.

Without CRM, in other words, true customer centricity cannot be achieved. Without CRM, it is impossible to collect and leverage the very data that allow customer-centric firms to thrive.

But it is important to point out that CRM alone does not make a company customer centric. It is not the solution to every customer-centric challenge. It is merely the first step—albeit a massively important step—toward customer-centric success.

Companies that do CRM correctly don't just *collect* data about their customers. Like Natasha, they also know how to use that data to serve those customers better. They align their marketing and sales strategies based on that data. They strive to reinforce relationships with their customers based on that data. And they constantly scrub that data and retest the initiatives built on that data to become ever-more effective purveyors of customer centricity.

CRM systems—whether extraordinarily complex like the massive system used at Tesco or elegantly simple like the stack of index cards used by Natasha—are the functionalities that enable us to determine the value of our customers; to segment those customers into cohorts according to their expected lifetime value; and to make better decisions about how, where, and on whom our marketing dollars should be spent. Every other action in a customer-centric company—the segmentation of the customer base, the highly focused and personalized marketing efforts, the ongoing relationship development between company and customer—is reliant upon the data collected via CRM.

CRM gives us nothing less than the most important and actionable information about all of our customers—their wants, their needs, their propensity to spend, their level of loyalty, their long-term value. CRM gives us knowledge, and it gives us power to influence, power to cajole, and power to *sell*.

No matter how big our CRM systems may grow, no matter how massive our customer base becomes, it remains paramount to understand on a very fundamental level that all of these efforts are about our companies' relationships with each and every customer we have—on a highly individualized level. It's not about mass marketing. It's not about company-wide promotions or seasonal sales. It's about relationships—specifically, strengthening relationships. That's what we're trying to get at, because only when we understand those relationships can we really begin to reap the benefits of all our customer-centric efforts.

So let us contrast this view of CRM with the standard definition that tells us CRM is a coordinated set of systems that a company uses to help create and extract more value from its customer base. What are the differences between these two perspectives? Well, the following key concerns regarding that standard definition help explain why CRM often fails to achieve its goals:

- The focus of a CRM effort should be less on systems and more on customers.

■ CRM efforts often (over)promise on value creation and extraction without proper understanding of the underlying behavioral patterns. Although it's great to want to create and extract value, this won't occur without a deep understanding of customer behavior.

■ CRM should not view the customer base as a mass of largely undifferentiated buyers; instead, managers need to celebrate heterogeneity to be truly customer centric.

Companies are just now beginning to understand some of these disconnects between what CRM generally offers and what they genuinely need. Unfortunately, this understanding has only arrived after years of CRM-related failings that, ultimately, have given CRM something of a bad reputation in the world of marketing.

Let me offer a personal example.

A few years ago, I became acquainted with a CEO of a large, well-known software company. As it turned out, this CEO was in the midst of installing a state-of-the-art CRM software system. Quite understandably, the CEO was excited about this new system, and given my expertise in this general area, he was eager to put me in touch with the information technology experts at his company who he thought were busy creating a system that would give the company a huge step forward toward customer centricity.

Unfortunately, the resulting conversation was a total disaster. I remember speaking to that CRM team and seeing blank stares on their faces as I talked about heterogeneity and customer lifetime value and customer equity. It became clear that we had very different views on what this system was supposed to ultimately achieve. Their goal was just to implement the system across the company. Presumably, smart decisions would follow automatically. The conversation went nowhere, and this CRM team successfully brainwashed the CEO to ensure that I wouldn't be allowed to meddle any further with their system-development plans.

It's a story I've seen unfold at companies all over the world, across all sectors, no matter how savvy the executives in charge or how cutting-edge the firms in question. And it's just one small example of why, by some estimates, up to 70% of companies who put CRM systems into place eventually deem their efforts to be failures.

That's a shockingly high number, of course. But there is a rather simple explanation for the failures. At some point, CRM became an end unto itself instead of a means to an end, that end being customer centricity. At some point, it was taken away from the marketers and salespeople and handed over almost entirely to the IT department. Almost inevitably, it devolved from a potentially groundbreaking strategic tool into a very expensive, very burdensome, and very disappointing exercise in systems engineering. Somehow, some way, all three of those letters lost their meaning, and CRM was no longer primarily focused on customers, relationships, or management.

So where do we draw the line? How do we know when CRM begins to lose its meaning in this manner? To answer these critical questions, let's turn back to Natasha. Let's think about the myriad measures that a CRM system can provide, and then let's ask ourselves which ones Natasha really needs in order to be customer centric and which ones are merely nice to know or are useful for other business purposes but not essential for customer centricity. A sample of 10 measures follows. Which of these measures are essential for customer centricity?

1. A red-flag warning that a particular customer is long overdue for her next appointment.

2. A red-flag warning that the supply of a particular hair-care product is running low.

3. The average CLV of all customers who have bought that hair-care product more than once.

4. Total sales associated with a Groupon promotion that Natasha tried last year.

5. Among new customers who first tried Natasha's services based on that promotion, the percentage that have made at least one repeat visit since then.

6. A breakdown of Natasha's revenue based on the use of credit cards versus checks versus cash.

7. The weighted average CLV of customers associated with each payment method.

8. The number of vacation days that her colorist, Yulia, took last year.

9. The number of customers who use Yulia but none of Natasha's other services.

10. The total revenue associated with Yulia's services last year.

Answer: all of the odd-numbered measures. Yes, some of the even-numbered ones may be important to Natasha's business as a whole, but not for the specific purpose of achieving or gauging customer centricity. Likewise, some of the odd-numbered measures are more essential than others, but all five share a common element in that they start to break down the customer base from a homogeneous mass into more distinct individuals with unique valuations.

Notice that some of the odd-numbered measures are pretty simple. Items like 1 and 9 are the kinds of issues that might be evident from a quick glance at Natasha's index cards. Others are more complex measures (e.g., the items involving CLV) that require much deeper insight or (more likely) some mathematical calculations beyond the raw "index card" data. This is where CRM starts to move from mere data collection to genuine value-added insight—a step that many companies don't fully appreciate.

Why Is CRM Just the First Step Toward Success in Customer Centricity?

I've had the opportunity to work with a great many people and companies who have spent a good deal of time stuck in the CRM mire, and when I ask them to describe their experience with CRM, the answers I get are shockingly consistent. And when I say shockingly consistent, I mean shockingly and consistently *negative*. I hear the word "disastrous." I hear "painful." I hear "clunky" and "burdensome." I rarely hear the word "wonderful." I rarely hear the world "earthshaking." I rarely even hear the word "useful."

In other words, CRM has fallen short of expectations. But the good news is, there are signs that it might soon get better.

After years of aimless and improper implementation, after countless companies have suffered bitter disappointment (if not major financial losses) on overbuilt and overexpansive CRM systems, the true sharps of marketing and the true experts of customer-centric practice are, slowly but surely, starting to bring CRM back to what it was meant to be in the first place: not the end-all, be-all of customer centricity, but rather just one crucially important step toward the achievement of customer-centric success.

Two years ago, had you spoken to anyone with even a passing understanding of or experience with CRM, your conversation would have likely been marked by the repeated use of the word "system." Today, you'll hear "interaction" and "recommendation," maybe even "nurture." You will hear, in other words, evidence that CRM is finally being recontextualized toward customer centricity.

Tesco, a company we first examined back in chapter 2, has been one of the firms carrying the torch for CRM, showing jaded marketers across all sectors that CRM really can work—provided, of course, that it is put to work properly, conceived of correctly, and viewed not as an end-all, be-all but rather as just one crucial element of a broader customer-centric strategy.

The Clubcard program on which Tesco's CRM strategy is built does *precisely* what customer-centric initiatives are supposed to do. The company knows exactly what kind of data it wants, finds unique and interesting ways to find that data, puts that data to use in ever-varied ways, and constantly asks itself whether it should be looking for new kinds of data—and whether the old data is still relevant. CRM has been massively important for Tesco's success. Maybe even central to that success. It is important to note, however, that the company has never viewed the Clubcard initiative—nor the CRM system behind it—as the solution to *all* of its customer-centric challenges.

Instead, Tesco sees the program as *enabling* technology—a means by which it can connect with individual customers in a very meaningful and intimate way; indeed, as the man most responsible for that program, founder of the company dunnhumby and renowned marketing consultant Clive Humby, told CustomerThink:[1]

> *When you start off with [the proper] mindset, it's not what can I do that will make a quick buck off the customer. It's what I can do that tells this customer I care about them. And because I care about them, they will stay with me for longer. I think the reason many CRM projects have a bad name is that they've been sold on the hype that knowing the customer was going to somehow magically make the customer more loyal. Well, it didn't. In fact, what it tended to do was show up the flaws in the business because it actually made it easier to do things badly for customers. It [CRM] automated call centers because you were a lower-value customer, and you couldn't get directly through to a person. Or it bombarded you with offers that you didn't*

1. "Tesco Shines at Loyalty: An Interview With Clive Humby," http://www.customerthink.com/interview/clive_humby_tesco_shines_at_loyalty

really want because it was cheap to send and you were
clearly a good prospect.

In other words, Humby is saying that when CRM
projects fail, they fail because after launching their
CRM systems, and after gathering tons of data about
their customers, companies eventually forget what
CRM was supposed to be in the first place. They forgot
that it's the individual customers and individual relationships that count—and that mass amounts of data
cannot be applied to massive amounts of customers.

So what is the lesson here? Even when incredible
amounts of incredibly valuable data is in hand, companies must always remember that the data are there
to serve a purpose: relationship-building first and sales
second. The gathering of data, in other words, is not
where the work ends. It's where it begins. And in the
realm of customer centricity, the companies that make
the effort to go beyond the basics are the ones that
survive and thrive.

Many very smart, very cutting-edge companies
have great products and services to sell. But the truly
customer-centric ones know their success is not based
just on those products and services; their success is
based, instead, on the means they use to *leverage* those
products and services—the things they do behind the
scenes through customer-centric strategy and CRM
know-how—to reinforce relationships with customers,

to understand the value of their customers, to identify the worthwhile ones and the dead weight, and to
build operations and systems that will allow them to
constantly fine-tune their understanding of the company's principal source of profits and growth.

No, not "the customer." But rather, *their customers*—
a broad mix of individuals, with different needs to
fulfill and different value to the company and different responsiveness to marketing action.

Conclusion

We began at a Nordstrom store in Fairbanks, Alaska. We'll conclude at a Nordstrom store a bit closer to home—or at least, a bit closer to *my* home.

It's a store I know quite well, because it's the store I've been going to for two decades since it first opened in the King of Prussia Mall. I am a very loyal Nordstrom shopper—probably among the most loyal in all of suburban Philadelphia. I go to Nordstrom for most of my casual pants, shirts, shoes, accessories, and my skin-care needs. And this doesn't include the thousands of dollars the rest of my family spends there every year as well. I like the designers that Nordstrom carries, I trust Nordstrom quality, and although I made light earlier of the company's customer-service fanaticism, I must admit, I do like the way I'm treated whenever I shop there. As a rule, the staff is friendly, helpful, and polite. But then again, they should be: I have been shopping there for years. The staff have seen me often enough to get to know me, and given our interactions, I don't doubt that my guys—the shoe guy and the pants guy and all the rest—really do know me.

It's just that Nordstrom—the company—doesn't know me very well.

And although this lack of knowledge has probably cost me a deal here or a special offer there, the reality is that the store's failure to really "get" me—their inability to really understand and leverage my value to them—is *their* loss. Not mine. Theirs.

I have a Nordstrom credit card, but I rarely use it; it's more convenient to stick with my regular Visa or MasterCard instead. So my purchases are spread out across all manners of payment that make it hard for them to get a complete picture of me. I belong to the Nordstrom customer loyalty program. Occasionally, I remember to ask for Nordstrom rewards points for my purchases. I have some kind of special status, but it reflects only a fraction of my Nordstrom purchases and doesn't seem particularly useful to me. I have spent a good deal of money on Nordstrom products over the years, and because I am a loyal Nordstrom customer, I will very likely continue spending on Nordstrom products well into the future. I will keep doing my part—more than my part, probably—to keep the store and the company profitable. Yet, in the end, I get almost nothing in return.

No matter what I do or don't do, I will be treated the same as pretty much every other customer who walks into that store—the same as the guy who has spent *half* as much money there as I have over the years, the same as the guy who is stepping into that store for the very first time, and the same as the guy who may one day drag in four used tires and demand a refund that he knows he doesn't deserve. The tire guy will get the same wonderful treatment that I'll get because as a customer at Nordstrom—no matter your ultimate worth, no matter your loyalty—you are treated like gold.

Which, as I'm sure you've figured out by now, is just flat-out wrong. It's not wrong because I, as a highly committed Nordstrom shopper, believe that I deserve better service and more attention than the tire guy (although I probably do). It's not wrong because I think I'm entitled to a little bit of coddling, not only from a particular Nordstrom employee in a particular store, but also from Nordstrom as a whole (although I probably do).

It's wrong because, as a marketing professor who is deeply interested in finding new and better ways of doing business, I absolutely know that Nordstrom, by treating me pretty much the same as everyone else, is missing a golden opportunity to do better for itself. By sticking to the tried-and-true rule of customer service, by treating each of their customers the same, by falling short of leveraging my loyalty for greater profits, Nordstrom, like countless other companies today, is wasting a golden opportunity. That opportunity, of course, is me: a very loyal, very committed, very bought-in customer who could easily be convinced to become an even better customer.

Yes, the shoe guy knows what kind of shoes I like, and yes, the pants guy knows what kind of pants I like. But I never get the sense that the shoe guy and the pants guy ever get together and figure out better ways of selling me on, for instance, package deals. I never get the sense that they coordinate their efforts and try to convince me when I go in for a new pair of pants that a new pair of shoes might also be a good idea. I never get the sense that that store is putting all of the information that they have (or *should* have) about me to work toward the very specific task of getting me to buy even more stuff—and again, I should emphasize, this would not be a hard sell. I'm already bought in—I just need a little nudge to buy in even more.

Alas, that nudge has yet to arrive. Or perhaps they've tried, but the nudge was so subtle that I never even noticed it.

Strictly from a marketing perspective, I must say, this situation is mildly frustrating. As an academic and customer-centric thinker, I know full well that I am *precisely* the kind of customer that Nordstrom should want. I am *precisely* the kind of customer that Nordstrom should target. I am *precisely* the kind of customer that can make that store more money and help it generate more profits for years and years to come. Yet Nordstrom just doesn't do enough to make that happen. But Nordstrom is hardly alone. Starbucks doesn't do enough. Costco doesn't do enough. Countless other companies don't do enough, either.

They don't do enough because they are all making the same basic strategic error: they continue to view and serve virtually all of their customers as "the customer."

By doing so, they are leaving money on the table.

We have covered a lot of ground in this book. We've talked about product centricity and its vulnerabilities in today's ultracompetitive business environment. We laid out a new definition of customer centricity and the surprising "paradox" that comes along with it. We explored the interplay between the competing notions of customer equity and brand equity. We detailed the flawed manner in which many companies have calculated the lifetime value of their customers—and then looked at how the simple notion of segmentation can help customer-centric companies get a much more accurate view of the value of their customer base. Finally, we examined the roots of customer relationship management, explained where CRM went wrong, and then tried to steer it right back toward its proper customer-centric course. These were all important topics.

But if there is just one lesson that I hope you'll take away from this book, it is this: if you fail to account for the unique behaviors and characteristics of each of your customers, and if you choose to ignore the indisputable reality of customer heterogeneity, then you are wasting an opportunity for greater, more lasting success.

Yes, the old product-centric model works. Yes, mass marketing works (and you don't hear a lot of people saying that these days). Yes, great customer service works. And yes, brands have tremendous staying power and can sometimes cut across customer segments and buoy profits even for the most product-centric of product-centric firms.

But despite all these well-established paths to profitability, there is still another option to consider: customer centricity. Even when we confront the reality that the road to customer centricity is not an easy one to travel, and even when we acknowledge that the most well-thought-out customer-centric programs may not bring equal benefits to all companies, it must also be said that the value that can be found by *really* understanding individual customers—their spending habits, their loyalty, their future potential—is simply too significant to be ignored.

You may have a remarkably successful company right now, and your company may well continue be remarkably successful far into the future, even if you change nothing—even if you continue on the most product-centric path. My contention, however, is simple: for many firms, in many markets, even greater success and even greater profits can be found through the tenets of customer centricity.

The Four Tenets of Customer Centricity

1. By recognizing the fundamental and inevitable differences among your customers, you can give your organization a strategic advantage over your product-centric competitors—who may know little to nothing about the customers who account for their success and survival.

2. By understanding that there is real and quantifiable value to be found in individual customers, you can better focus your long-term marketing efforts on precisely those customers who will generate the greatest long-term value.

3. By working to quantify the value of each and every one of your customers, you can gain enormously valuable insight about how much you should be willing to spend to keep an existing customer and how much you should be willing to spend to acquire a new customer.

4. By moving forward with a highly focused customer relationship management initiative, you can gather and leverage even more information about your customers who will allow your company to serve those customers in a more personalized (yet genuine) manner than any competitor can.

In other words, by simply stepping back and breaking away from that old, increasingly vulnerable idea that "the customer is always right"—by being willing to endure the short-term pains of restructuring your organization to target the right customers—you can create a hedge against the inevitable pressures of today's business world: commoditization, technology, globalization, deregulation, and of course, unyielding, ever-building competition.

Customer centricity gives you an advantage. It creates opportunity. It opens new doors.

It is a sound, proven, winning strategy—and no, it's not about just being "nice" to your customers. It's not about taking back used tires you didn't sell in the first place. It's not about customer service at all, really, at least not in the traditional sense. Customer centricity, more than anything else, is about targeting the right customers in the right way to generate the right results.

Customer centricity is about leaving old thinking and old practices behind. Customer centricity is about creating smarter, more strategically focused organizations. Customer centricity is about leveraging the single most valuable asset that your company has: your customers.

They are out there, waiting to be served. But they don't all expect, require, or *deserve* the same level of service or attention. Ignore their heterogeneous needs—and their heterogeneous value to your company—at your own risk.

Acknowledgments

Customer centricity is all about thoughtful collaboration—and this is true whether you are implementing it as a senior executive in a company or a marketing professor writing about it. In the case of the executive, it is all about surrounding the customer with the right products, services, and recommendations; for the professor, it is all about surrounding yourself with the right colleagues, co-authors, and students. I am thankful that I have been blanketed by the best of all of these collaborators at The Wharton School. Much of this book is directly attributable to the many things I have learned from my teaching, research, and consulting experiences. Particular thanks go to my long-time co-author Bruce Hardie from the London Business School, whose scholarly excellence and extraordinarily high standards have made me a better researcher; Renana Peres from Hebrew University in Jerusalem who first exposed me to many of these issues in developing a new course that we taught together at Wharton (for instance, she deserves credit for helping me frame CRM through the "Natasha" story and for inspiring many of the other ideas expressed here); my colleague and friend Eric Bradlow and the staff of the Wharton Customer Analytics Initiative, who bring many of these concepts to life with top companies from around the world; the many past students from my quirky elective courses (MKTG 775 and MKTG 476/776) who have helped me "spread the gospel" about these ideas with great passion and enthusiasm; and Tim Hyland of Drexel University, who watched countless hours of videos from those courses to turn my scattered lessons into the well-organized words on the pages here. And last but not least is my family: Mina, Shayna, and Corey—my ultimate collaborators, who help keep me very centered around what matters most in life.

Index

121

About the Author

Peter S. Fader is the Frances and Pei-Yuan Chia Professor of Marketing at the Wharton School of the University of Pennsylvania. He is also the co-director of the Wharton Customer Analytics Initiative, an academic research center focused on fostering productive collaborations between data-driven firms and top academic researchers around the world.

Fader's research is based on the analysis of behavioral data to understand and forecast customer shopping and purchasing activities. He works with firms from a wide range of industries, such as consumer packaged goods, interactive media, financial services, and pharmaceuticals; much of his work highlights common patterns that arise across these seemingly unrelated industries.

Fader has been quoted or featured in *The New York Times, Wall Street Journal, The Economist, The Washington Post,* and on NPR, among other media. He has also won many awards for his teaching and research accomplishments. In 2009, Fader was named a "Professor to Watch" by the *Financial Times,* which discussed his interest in "the swathes of hard data consumers generate through their spending habits." He is also on the editorial board of a number of leading journals, including *Marketing Science, Journal of Marketing Research,* and *Journal of Interactive Marketing.*

About Wharton Digital Press

Wharton Digital Press was established to inspire bold, insightful thinking within the global business community. In the tradition of The Wharton School of the University of Pennsylvania and its online business journal *Knowledge@Wharton*, Wharton Digital Press uses innovative digital technologies to help managers meet the challenges of today and tomorrow.

As an entrepreneurial publisher, Wharton Digital Press delivers relevant, accessible, conceptually sound, and empirically based business knowledge to readers wherever and whenever they need it. Its format ranges from ebooks and enhanced ebooks to mobile apps and print books available through print-on-demand technology. Directed to a general business audience, the Press's areas of interest include management and strategy, innovation and entrepreneurship, finance and investment, leadership, marketing, operations, human resources, social responsibility, business-government relations, and more.

http://wdp.wharton.upenn.edu

About The Wharton School

The Wharton School of the University of Pennsylvania—founded in 1881 as the first collegiate business school—is recognized globally for intellectual leadership and ongoing innovation across every major discipline of business education. The most comprehensive source of business knowledge in the world, Wharton bridges research and practice through its broad engagement with the global business community. The School has more than 4,800 undergraduate, MBA, executive MBA, and doctoral students; more than 9,000 annual participants in executive education programs; and an alumni network of 86,000 graduates.

http://www.wharton.upenn.edu

CPSIA information can be obtained at www.ICGtesting.com
Printed in the USA
BVOW041707190312

285556BV00001B/73/P

9 781613 630075